Englische Laute			
Mitlaute (Konsonanten)			
[b]	**b**ed	[p]	**p**icture
[d]	**d**ay	[r]	**r**ed
[ð]	**th**e	[s]	**s**ix
[f]	**f**amily	[ʃ]	**sh**e
[g]	**g**o	[t]	**t**en
[ŋ]	morni**ng**	[tʃ]	**ch**air
[h]	**h**ouse	[v]	**v**ideo
[j]	**y**ou	[w]	**w**e, **o**ne
[k]	**c**an, mil**k**	[z]	ea**s**y
[l]	**l**etter	[ʒ]	revi**s**ion
[m]	**m**an	[dʒ]	**p**a**g**e
[n]	**n**o	[θ]	**th**ank you
Selbstlaute (Vokale)			
[ɑː]	c**a**r	[i]	happ**y**
[æ]	**a**pple	[iː]	t**ea**cher
[e]	p**e**n	[ɒ]	d**o**g
[ə]	**a**gain	[ɔː]	b**a**ll
[ɜː]	g**ir**l	[ʊ]	b**oo**k
[ʌ]	b**u**t	[u]	Jan**u**ary
[ɪ]	**i**t	[uː]	t**oo**, tw**o**
Doppellaute			
[aɪ]	**I**, m**y**	[ɪə]	h**ere**, id**ea**
[aʊ]	n**ow**, m**ou**se	[əʊ]	hell**o**
[eɪ]	n**a**me, th**ey**	[ɔɪ]	b**oy**
[eə]	th**ere**, p**air**	[ʊə]	s**ure**

[ː] der vorangehende Laut ist lang, z. B. *you* [juː]

[‿] der Bindebogen zeigt, dass zwei Wörter in der Aussprache verbunden werden

['] die folgende Silbe trägt den Hauptakzent

[ˌ] die folgende Silbe trägt den Nebenakzent

Unit 1 On the move

> **Tip**
>
> Welcome back! Du kommst sicher gut erholt aus den Sommerferien. Vielleicht hast du sogar im Urlaub ab und zu Englisch gesprochen? Um Schritt für Schritt wieder ins Englischlernen einzusteigen, kannst du jeden Tag ein paar zufällig ausgewählte Vokabeln wiederholen: Zieh einfach einige Karten aus deiner Kartei oder schließ die Augen und tippe mit dem Finger auf die Vokabellisten im Heft oder Buch.

Introduction

on the move [ˌɒn ðə ˈmuːv]	unterwegs
travelling *(no pl)* [ˈtrævlɪŋ]	(das) Reisen
foreign [ˈfɒrɪn]	ausländisch; fremd
seasick [ˈsiːsɪk]	seekrank
luggage *(no pl)* [ˈlʌgɪdʒ]	Gepäck
to **be afraid (of)** [bɪ əˈfreɪd əv]	(sich) fürchten; Angst haben (vor)
plane [pleɪn]	Flugzeug
departure lounge [dɪˈpɑːtʃə ˌlaʊndʒ]	Abflughalle
passport [ˈpɑːspɔːt]	Pass; Reisepass
boarding card [ˈbɔːdɪŋ ˌkɑːd]	Bordkarte
desk [desk]	Schalter
visa [ˈviːzə], **visas** [ˈviːzəz] *(pl)*	Visum, Visa *(Pl.)*; Einreisebewilligung
passenger [ˈpæsndʒə]	Passagier/-in; Fahrgast
flight attendant [ˈflaɪt əˌtendnt]	Flugbegleiter/-in
customs *(sg)* [ˈkʌstəmz]	Zoll

Green Line **4** G9

Vokabellernheft

von
Martina Nolte-Bohres

herausgegeben von
Harald Weisshaar

Ernst Klett Verlag
Stuttgart · Leipzig

Vorwort

Liebe Schülerin, lieber Schüler,

in den vergangenen drei Schuljahren hast du eine ganze Menge Vokabeln gelernt und dir so schon einen beachtlichen englischen Wortschatz angeeignet. Das Green Line 4 Vokabellernheft  unterstützt dich dabei, diesen im 8. Schuljahr noch zu erweitern. Du kannst mit dem Vokabellernheft den gesamten Lernwortschatz wiederholen und üben, und das nicht nur zu Hause, sondern auch unterwegs, denn es passt in deine Hosentasche. Durch die Gliederung der Vokabeln nach den Buchteilen verlierst du nie den Überblick darüber, welche Wörter du schon kannst und welche du dir noch einmal anschauen musst. Tipps zum Vokabellernen findest du zu Beginn jeder Unit.

Zusätzlich zum Wortschatz bietet dir dein Vokabellernheft auch abwechslungsreiche Übungen, in denen du die gelernten Wörter direkt nach jedem Abschnitt anwendest. Dies hilft dir dabei, die Vokabeln gut zu behalten, und bereitet dich gleichzeitig auf Tests vor. Am Ende jeder Unit bzw. Text smart gibt es eine Übung zur Selbstkontrolle (Check on your …), mit der du herausfinden kannst, wie fit du in einem bestimmten Thema bist.

Markiere beim Lernen alle Wörter und Wendungen, die du dir nicht so gut merken kannst, mit einem Bleistift. Wiederhole sie dann in regelmäßigen Abständen.

Mit den Lösungen auf den Seiten 73 bis 80 überprüfst du dich schließlich selbst.

Viel Spaß und Erfolg mit deinem Vokabellernheft!

Dein Green Line Team

suitcase ['suːtkeɪs]	Koffer
ferry ['feri]	Fähre
control [kən'trəʊl]	Kontrolle
arrivals hall [ə'raɪvlz ˌhɔːl]	Ankunftshalle
currency ['kʌrnsi]	Währung
duty-free [ˌdjuːtiˈfriː]	zollfrei

1 Find the word

Write down the answers to the questions and find the solution.

1. What is a person called who is travelling by plane, bus or train?

2. Where do you go after your plane has landed and you've picked up your luggage?

3. How might you feel when you're travelling on a ship in bad weather?

4. What do you call money that is different from the money in your country? foreign ▢▢▢▢▢▢▢▢

5. What do you use to put your clothes in before you go on a trip?

Solution: Let's go by ▢▢▢▢▢ !

1

Station 1: You told us there was free wifi!

athletics *(no pl)* [æθ'letɪks]	Leichtathletik
vending machine ['vendɪŋ məˌʃiːn]	Automat
to **spill** [spɪl], **spilt** [spɪlt], **spilt** [spɪlt]	verschütten; auslaufen
to **hang on** [ˌhæŋ 'ɒn]	(einen Augenblick) warten
coast [kəʊst]	Küste
shutter ['ʃʌtə]	Fensterladen
abroad [ə'brɔːd]	im Ausland; ins Ausland
groan [grəʊn]	Stöhnen
hostel ['hɒstl]	Herberge
addict ['ædɪkt]	Süchtige/-r; Abhängige/-r
to **mutter** ['mʌtə]	murmeln
latest ['leɪtɪst]	neueste/-r/-s
closed [kləʊzd]	geschlossen; zu
big deal [bɪg 'diːl]	große Sache
apart from [ə'pɑːt frəm]	abgesehen von; außer
soup [suːp]	Suppe
herb [hɜːb]	Kraut
garlic ['gɑːlɪk]	Knoblauch
style [staɪl]	Stil
to **be called** [bi 'kɔːld]	heißen; genannt werden
sleep [sliːp]	Schlaf

2 Rhymes

Find the rhyming words. They're all new in Station 1.

1. mutter – _____
2. toast – _____
3. group – _____
4. deep – _____
5. fill – _____
6. mile – _____

3 Say it in a different way

Write down the missing word or phrase to make a sentence with a similar meaning.

1. Just a moment, I'll send my brother a message.

   _____, I'll send my brother a message.

2. I'd like to work in a different country.

   I'd like to work _____.

3. Steve thinks he can't live without his phone.

   Steve is a phone _____.

4. What's your sister's name?

   What's _____?

5. You should go to bed now.

   You should get some _____.

6. My friend's clothes are really special.

   My friend has got her own _____.

7. Lunch seems to be very important in France.

   Lunch seems to be a _____ in France.

Station 2: Idiot nephew?

nephew [ˈnefjuː]	Neffe
although [ɔːlˈðəʊ]	obwohl
purpose [ˈpɜːpəs]	Ziel; Absicht; Zweck
date of birth [ˌdeɪt əv ˈbɜːθ]	Geburtsdatum
suspicious [səˈspɪʃəs]	misstrauisch; argwöhnisch
side room [ˈsaɪd ˌruːm]	Nebenraum
security [sɪˈkjʊərəti]	Sicherheit; Schutz; Wachdienst
immigration office [ˌɪmɪˈgreɪʃn ˌɒfɪs]	Einwanderungsbehörde
immigration [ˌɪmɪˈgreɪʃn]	Immigration; Einwanderung; Einreise
truth [truːθ]	Wahrheit
quite [kwaɪt]	ziemlich; ganz; völlig
traffic [ˈtræfɪk]	Verkehr
to **search for** [ˈsɜːtʃ fə]	suchen (nach)
traveller [ˈtrævlə]	Reisende/-r
to **bother** [ˈbɒðə]	stören; belästigen
to **suggest** [səˈdʒest]	vorschlagen
chewing gum [ˈtʃuːɪŋ ˌgʌm]	Kaugummi
take-off [ˈteɪk ɒf]	Start; Abheben
landing [ˈlændɪŋ]	Landung
out of [ˈaʊt əv]	aus … heraus
to **contain** [kənˈteɪn]	enthalten
gate [geɪt]	Gate; Flugsteig; Ausgang
delay [dɪˈleɪ]	Verzögerung; Verspätung

4 Word friends

Make pairs of two nouns and write them down.

room   hall   immigration   flight   machine
side   office   vending   arrivals   attendant

1. _____
2. _____
3. _____
4. _____
5. _____

5 Airport words

Write down four airport nouns for each part of the grid.

People at the airport	Places at the airport

Story: Where I belong

where I belong [ˌweərˌaɪ bɪˈlɒŋ]	wo ich hingehöre
responsible [rɪsˈpɒnsəbl]	verantwortlich; verantwortungsvoll
to **accept** [əkˈsept]	akzeptieren; hinnehmen; annehmen
mask [mɑːsk]	Maske
smuggler [ˈsmʌglə]	Schmuggler/-in
overloaded [ˌəʊvəˈləʊdɪd]	überladen
shark [ʃɑːk]	Hai
crushed [krʌʃt]	eingequetscht; eingeklemmt
to **rock** [rɒk]	schaukeln
to **smash** [smæʃ]	zerschlagen; zerschmettern
to **be sick** [bi ˈsɪk]	sich übergeben
to **close oneself away from** [ˌkləʊz əˈweɪ frəm]	sich abschotten von
to **give sb a piggyback** [gɪv ə ˈpɪgibæk]	jmdn. Huckepack nehmen
checkpoint [ˈtʃekpɔɪnt]	Kontrollpunkt
seat [siːt]	Sitz; Sitzplatz
except [ɪkˈsept]	außer; bis auf
air-conditioning [ˌeəkənˈdɪʃnɪŋ]	Klimaanlage
to **concentrate** [ˈkɒnsntreɪt]	(sich) konzentrieren
rain [reɪn]	Regen
steady [ˈstedi]	kontinuierlich; unaufhörlich
depressing [dɪˈpresɪŋ]	deprimierend; bedrückend
drizzle [ˈdrɪzl]	Nieselregen
ground [graʊnd]	Boden; Erdboden
to **cover** [ˈkʌvə]	abdecken; bedecken; zudecken
concrete [ˈkɒŋkriːt]	Beton
official [əˈfɪʃl]	Beamte/-r
to **pretend** [prɪˈtend]	vortäuschen; tun als ob

useless ['juːsləs]	nutzlos
invisible [ɪnˈvɪzəbl]	unsichtbar
phone box [ˈfəʊn ˌbɒks]	Telefonzelle
to **fetch** [fetʃ]	holen; abholen
button [ˈbʌtn]	Knopf
Somali [səˈmɑːli]	Somali
straight [streɪt]	gerade; direkt; geradewegs
refugee [ˌrefjʊˈdʒiː]	Flüchtling
climate [ˈklaɪmət]	Klima
to **be homesick** [bi ˈhəʊmsɪk]	Heimweh haben

6 A refugee's story

Put in the correct adjectives. They're all new on pages 16–18 in your book.

I came here on an _____ boat. There were

so many people on it that I was _____

between an old man and a boy. When I arrived in England,

it was raining. It was a _____ drizzle

that didn't stop for days. For me, this weather was really

_____ – I felt sad because I missed the sun.

And I was _____ too! I wanted to go back

and be with my family, but I knew I couldn't.

7 Mixed bag: Travel words

Put in the correct words. Make sure you use the correct tense for the verbs.

official | to rock | checkpoints | seasick | landing
air-conditioning | passport | ferry | take-off

1. I went to Britain by _____. The weather was bad, so the ship _____ badly and I felt _____.

2. On our trip to Egypt we had to go through several _____. At the last one, I couldn't find my _____ at first. I was lucky that the _____ was very nice – he waited until I found it.

3. When I'm on a plane, I always use chewing-gum during _____ and _____ so that my ears don't hurt. I always take a sweatshirt with me too because at the airport I often feel cold in the _____.

Action UK! The guitar lesson

guitar [gɪˈtɑː]	Gitarre
I go wherever the wind takes me. [aɪ ˌgəʊ weəˌrevə ðə wɪnd ˈteɪks miː]	Ich lasse mich treiben.
future [ˈfjuːtʃə]	zukünftig
origin [ˈɒrɪdʒɪn]	Ursprung; Herkunft; Abstammung
destination [ˌdestɪˈneɪʃn]	Ziel; Reiseziel
outgoing [aʊtˈgəʊɪŋ]	kontaktfreudig
easy-going [ˌiːziˈgəʊɪŋ]	locker; unkompliziert
odd [ɒd]	seltsam; komisch
to be set (in) [bi ˈset ɪn]	spielen (in); seinen Schauplatz haben (in)
unreal [ˌʌnˈrɪəl]	irreal
specific [spəˈsɪfɪk]	spezifisch; speziell
era [ˈɪərə]	Ära; Zeitalter
lavish [ˈlævɪʃ]	üppig; verschwenderisch
magic [ˈmædʒɪk]	Magie; Zauberei
supernatural [ˈsuːpəˌnætʃrl]	übernatürlich
force [fɔːs]	Kraft; Macht
mythical [ˈmɪθɪkl]	sagenhaft; sagenumwoben

8 Odd word out

Cross out the word that doesn't fit.

1. guitar | drums | recorder | mask
2. invisible | outgoing | laid-back | easy-going
3. magic | supernatural | concrete | wizard
4. destination | truth | journey | traveller
5. unreal | mythical | magical | realistic

9 Film genres

Draw lines to match the film genres with their main elements.

1. fantasy
2. science fiction
3. romance
4. historical

a) inventions in science, often set in the future
b) set in specific historical era, often lavish costumes
c) magic / supernatural forces
d) love, relationships, often happy ending

10 Check on your ... adjectives for a person's character

Make a list of adjectives that are useful to describe somebody's character.

_____

_____

_____

_____

_____

_____

_____

_____

Skills: How to tell a travel story

the other day [ðiˌʌðə ˈdeɪ]	neulich
It turned out that ... [ɪt ˌtɜːndˈaʊt ðæt]	Es stellte sich heraus, dass ...
war [wɔː]	Krieg
Egyptian [ɪˈdʒɪpʃn]	Ägypter/-in; ägyptisch
dominoes [ˈdɒmɪnəʊz]	Domino
to **order** [ˈɔːdə]	bestellen
Arab [ˈærəb]	arabisch

Unit task: True or not true?

convincing [kənˈvɪnsɪŋ]	überzeugend

1 What can you say?

You tell your cousin about a new friend you made.
Write it down in English.

1. Du erzählst, dass du neulich mit deinen Eltern in ein ägyptisches Restaurant gegangen bist.

   _____

   _____

2. Du sagst, dass ihr euch mit dem Chef und seinem Sohn unterhalten habt und es sich herausstellte, dass sein Sohn, Ahmed, auf deine Schule geht.

   _____

   _____

3. Du erzählst, dass Ahmed ein arabischer Freund von dir ist.

   _____

AC 1

Across cultures 1 Dos and don'ts

> **Tip**
>
> Hast du eine Vokabelkartei? Dann mach doch einfach mal Stichproben: Ziehe zehn beliebige Karten aus dem Wortschatz der vergangenen beiden Schuljahre heraus und überprüfe, ob du die Wörter noch weißt. Falls dir nicht alle sofort einfallen, überlege dir Merkhilfen, die du auf den Karten notieren kannst.

dos and don'ts [ˌduːz ənd ˈdəʊnts]	Ge- und Verbote; was man tun und was man nicht tun sollte
behaviour *(no pl)* [bɪˈheɪvjə]	Verhalten; Benehmen; Betragen
point at sb/sth [ˈpɔɪnt æt]	mit dem Finger auf jmdn./etw. zeigen
to **stand in the way of sb/sth** [ˌstænd ɪn ðə ˈweɪ əv]	jmdm./etw. im Weg stehen
to **hold open** [ˌhəʊld ˈəʊpn]	aufhalten
to **talk with your mouth full** [ˌtɔːk wɪð jɔː ˈmaʊθ fʊl]	mit vollem Mund sprechen
to **litter** [ˈlɪtə]	verschmutzen; verunreinigen; Müll herumliegen lassen
ear [ɪə]	Ohr
to **guess** [ɡes]	annehmen
custom [ˈkʌstəm]	Gewohnheit; Brauch; Sitte
ice breaker [ˈaɪsˌbreɪkə]	Eisbrecher *(Sätze, um mit jmdm. ins Gespräch zu kommen)*
glad [ɡlæd]	froh
crowded [ˈkraʊdɪd]	überfüllt

AC 1

leaflet [ˈliːflət]	Broschüre; Informationsblatt; Prospekt
manners *(pl)* [ˈmænəz]	Manieren; Benehmen

1 Good manners or not?

Write the phrases in the correct part of the grid.

`talk with your mouth full`   `point at somebody`   `say hello back`

`hold the door open for others`

`say 'please' and 'thank you'`

`litter the park`

`smile at others`

`stand in the way`

Good manners	Bad manners

Text smart 1 Drama

> **Tip**
>
> Warte mit dem Vokabellernen nicht bis zum letzten Moment. Verteile die Wörter, die du lernen musst, lieber möglichst gleichmäßig auf die Zeit, die dir zur Verfügung steht. Lege Pausen ein, in denen du eine andere Hausaufgabe machst oder dich auch mal ausruhst.

Introduction

to **entertain** [ˌentəˈteɪn]	unterhalten
to **stage** [steɪdʒ]	aufführen
to **mess sth up** [ˌmesˈʌp]	etw. durcheinanderbringen; etw. vergeigen
performance [pəˈfɔːməns]	Aufführung; Vorstellung
director [dɪˈrektə]	Regisseur/-in
lines *(pl)* [laɪnz]	Text
protagonist [prəʊˈtægnɪst]	Protagonist/-in; Hauptfigur

1 What a director says …

Put in the correct verbs.

identify with | stage | mess up | get into | entertain

1. This year, we're going to _____ *Claire's Devil*.

2. First, everybody needs to _____ character.

3. So try to _____ your role.

4. Remember: We want to _____ the audience!

5. Learn your lines – don't _____ the performance.

Station 1

devil [ˈdevl]	Teufel
teenage [ˈtiːneɪdʒ]	jugendlich; Jugend-
dilemma [daɪˈlemə]	Dilemma; Zwickmühle
to **face** [feɪs]	gegenüber stehen; konfrontiert werden mit
angel [ˈeɪndʒl]	Engel
to **phone** [fəʊn]	anrufen; telefonieren
tonight [təˈnaɪt]	heute Abend; heute Nacht
conscience [ˈkɒnʃns]	Gewissen
motivation [ˌməʊtɪˈveɪʃn]	Motivation; Beweggründe
unsure [ʌnˈʃʊə]	unsicher
convinced [kənˈvɪnst]	überzeugt
tempted [ˈtemptɪd]	in Versuchung gebracht
to **tempt** [tempt]	in Versuchung führen; reizen

2 Opposites

Find the opposite of each word.

1. angel   ↪ _____

2. this morning ↪ _____

3. sure   ↪ _____

4. real   ↪ _____

5. shy   ↪ _____

6. useful ↪ _____

TS 1

Station 2

motive [ˈməʊtɪv]	Motiv; Beweggrund
to **take a risk** [ˌteɪk ə ˈrɪsk]	ein Risiko eingehen
to **exaggerate** [ɪgˈzædʒəreɪt]	übertreiben
sensible [ˈsensɪbl]	vernünftig
Let's face it. [lets ˈfeɪs ɪt]	Machen wir uns doch nichts vor.
white lie [ˌwaɪt ˈlaɪ]	Notlüge
mean [miːn]	gemein
pushy [ˈpʊʃi]	aufdringlich; penetrant; aggressiv
argument [ˈɑːgjəmənt]	Argument
tempting [ˈtemptɪŋ]	verführerisch

3 Definitions

Put in the correct words.

1. A _____ is the reason why somebody does something.

2. A _____ is a small lie you use when you don't want to hurt a person's feelings.

3. You're _____ when you really get on somebody's nerves to get what you want.

4. You use _____ to explain your reasons for your opinion.

5. A _____ person is someone who is really nasty.

Station 3

to **warn** [wɔːn]	warnen
hardly [ˈhɑːdli]	kaum
dishonest [dɪˈsɒnɪst]	unehrlich
to **do well** [ˌduː ˈwel]	gute Leistungen erbringen
schoolwork [ˈskuːlwɜːk]	Schularbeiten
bit by bit [ˌbɪt baɪ ˈbɪt]	Stück für Stück
fake [feɪk]	falsch; gefälscht

4 Mixed bag: Claire's thoughts

Put in the correct words or phrases.
Make sure you use the correct tense for the verbs.

sensible | dishonest | Let's face it | do well | warn | tempting

Mum _____ me of Rob …

Well, she isn't completely wrong.

_____ – he tempted me

to be _____, and now

I feel bad. But on the other hand it's so

_____ to go to the party … And usually I'm

very _____ – I work hard at school and I always

_____ in tests …

TS 1

Station 4

youth [ju:θ]	Jugend
to support [sə'pɔ:t]	unterstützen
tolerant ['tɒlrnt]	tolerant
There's no need to … [ˌðeəz nəʊ 'ni:d tə]	Es gibt keinen Grund zu …
to expect [ɪk'spekt]	erwarten
to ring [rɪŋ], rang [ræŋ], rung [rʌŋ]	anrufen
out of order [ˌaʊt əv 'ɔ:də]	kaputt; außer Betrieb
shocked [ʃɒkt]	schockiert; geschockt
guilty ['gɪlti]	schuldig

Options

casting ['kɑ:stɪŋ]	Casting; Rollenbesetzung

5 Describe feelings and behaviour

Put in adjectives from Stations 3 and 4.

1. Claire's mum would be _____ if she knew that Claire had lied to her.

2. On the one hand Claire feels _____, but on the other hand she wants to have fun.

3. Claire thinks that her parents could be more _____.

4. Claire knows she shouldn't be _____, but she still lies to her parents.

TS 1

6 Jumbled sentences

Find the right word order and make sentences.

1. order   is   our   of   phone   out

   _____

2. no   worry   need   to   there's

   _____

3. leads   always   lie   another   one   to

   _____

7 Check on your ... irregular verbs

Look at the irregular verbs that you know by now. Make sure you know all three forms.
Write down those verbs you'd like to practise.

_____

_____

_____

_____

_____

_____

_____

_____

AC 2

Across cultures 2 The USA: Country of contrasts

> **Tip**
>
> Lerne neue Wörter und Redewendungen auch weiterhin im Satzzusammenhang, wenn es wichtig ist, die passenden Ergänzungen zu kennen oder zu wissen, mit welchen grammatischen Strukturen man die Wörter verwendet. Notiere dir Beispiele wie: *to go* swimming, home, away, to school, *I like* reading, playing football, playing the drums, *I'd rather go* home, *watch* the film on TV

contrast ['kɒntrɑːst]	Kontrast; Unterschied; Gegensatz
the US (= the United States) [ðə juːˈes]	die USA (= die Vereinigten Staaten)
urban ['ɜːbn]	städtisch; Stadt-
endless ['endləs]	endlos
sparse [spɑːs]	dünn; spärlich
populated ['pɒpjəleɪtɪd]	bevölkert; besiedelt
rural ['rʊərl]	ländlich
single ['sɪŋgl]	einzeln; einzig; alleinstehend
tractor ['træktə]	Traktor
desert ['dezət]	Wüste
(the) Southwest [ˌsaʊθˈwest]	(der) Südwesten; im Südwesten; südwestlich
temperature ['temprətʃə]	Temperatur
degree Fahrenheit (°F) ['færnhaɪt]	Grad Fahrenheit
cactus ['kæktəs]	Kaktus
cool [kuːl]	kühl
zone [zəʊn]	Zone
immigrant ['ɪmɪgrənt]	Immigrant/-in; Einwanderer/-in

AC 2

European [jʊərə'piːən]	Europäer/-in; europäisch; aus Europa
cultural ['kʌltʃrl]	kulturell
redwood (tree) ['redwʊd ˌtriː]	Mammutbaum
foot [fʊt], **feet** [fiːt] *(pl)*	Fuß *(Längenmaß: 30,48 cm)*
skyscraper ['skaɪskreɪpə]	Wolkenkratzer
state [steɪt]	Staat; Bundesstaat; Land
to **fly** [flaɪ], **flew** [fluː], **flown** [fləʊn]	hissen
a (day/week/year) [ə 'deɪ/wiːk/jɪə]	pro (Tag/Woche/Jahr)
population [ˌpɒpjə'leɪʃn]	Bevölkerung; Population
billionaire ['bɪliəneə]	Milliardär/-in
scenery ['siːnri]	Landschaft
simply ['sɪmpli]	einfach nur
dense [dens]	dicht
in the country [ˌɪn ðə 'kʌntri]	auf dem Land
mountainous ['maʊntɪnəs]	bergig
flat [flæt]	flach; platt
gigantic [dʒaɪ'gæntɪk]	gigantisch; riesig
wealthy ['welθi]	wohlhabend; reich
wasteful ['weɪstfl]	verschwenderisch
luxury ['lʌkʃri]	Luxus
to **represent** [ˌreprɪ'zent]	repräsentieren; darstellen; stehen für
to **symbolize** *(AE)* ['sɪmbəlaɪz]	symbolisieren
harsh [hɑːʃ]	rau; hart
extreme [ɪk'striːm]	extrem; radikal
standard of living [ˌstændəd ˌəv 'lɪvɪŋ]	Lebensstandard
to **become friends** [bɪˌkʌm ˌ'frendz]	sich anfreunden; Freundschaft schließen

AC 2

vacation (AE) [vəˈkeɪʃn]	Ferien; Urlaub
dude (coll) [duːd]	Mann; Alter (ugs.)
awesome [ˈɔːsəm]	super; spitze
US [juːˈes]	US-amerikanisch
to **have no clue** [ˌhæv nəʊ ˈkluː]	keine Ahnung haben
route planner [ˈruːt ˌplænə]	Routenplaner
Brit [brɪt]	Brite/Britin (ugs.)
colonist [ˈkɒlənɪst]	Siedler/-in; Kolonist/-in
corn [kɔːn]	Korn; Mais; Getreide
wheat [wiːt]	Weizen
to **ride** [raɪd], **rode** [rəʊd], **ridden** [ˈrɪdn]	fahren; reiten
epic [ˈepɪk]	episch; *hier:* geil
massive [ˈmæsɪv]	riesig; massiv; *hier:* super
complete [kəmˈpliːt]	vollständig; komplett; völlig

1 Contrasts in the US

Put in the correct opposites.

1. In _____ areas, you have a huge choice of shops, theatres or restaurants, but you find fewer open spaces than in _____ areas.

2. There are many _____ or even rich people in the US – 10 million millionaires is a really large number! But many Americans are _____: They don't have enough money although they have two jobs or more.

AC 2

3. Cities are _____ populated. When people from New York come to the _____ populated Midwest, they often feel like they're in a different world.

2 Word groups: Rural or urban?

Write the words or phrases in the correct part of the grid.

crowded   parks   endless   corn   taxi   scenery
wheat   skyscraper   redwood tree   Broadway plays
cactus   tractor   densely populated   noisy

In the city	In the country

AC 2

3 That's the US!

Put in the correct adjectives.

extreme | awesome | cultural | rural | European | harsh

Tristan: Many _____ immigrants came to the US in the 19th and 20th centuries. My family came from London.

Callum: So you're a Brit! Maybe there aren't that many _____ differences between you and me …

Tristan: No, dude! We're going to have an _____ time together, I'm sure.

Callum: I hope it'll be warmer in California than in London.

Tristan: I bet it will. Sometimes we have really _____ temperatures here. Too hot, even for me!

Callum: But there are also areas in the US which have a really _____ climate …

Tristan: But you aren't going to Alaska, are you?! It's much too _____ anyway, at least for me!

Unit 2 Kids in America

> **Tip**
>
> Bei Wörtern wie *exaggerated* kannst du dir vielleicht nicht sofort ihre Schreibung genau merken. In solchen Fällen hilft es, sie mehrmals hintereinander aufzuschreiben und die Buchstabenfolge laut aufzusagen.

kid [kɪd]	Jugendliche/-r; Kind

Introduction

impression [ɪmˈpreʃn]	Impression; Eindruck
orientation [ˌɔːriənˈteɪʃn]	Orientierung; Orientierungs-
to **give a talk** [ˌɡɪv ə ˈtɔːk]	einen Vortrag halten
suburb [ˈsʌbɜːb]	Vorort
suburban [səˈbɜːbn]	Vorstadt-
front yard *(AE)* [ˌfrʌnt ˈjɑːd]	Vorgarten
shopping mall [ˈʃɒpɪŋ ˌmɔːl]	Einkaufszentrum
middle school *(AE)* [ˈmɪdl ˌskuːl]	Mittelschule *(weiterführende Schule in den USA, Mittelstufe)*
high school *(AE)* [ˈhaɪ ˌskuːl]	High School *(weiterführende Schule in den USA, Oberstufe)*
hallway [ˈhɔːlweɪ]	Flur; Diele; Korridor
hall pass [ˈhɔːl pɑːs]	*Erlaubnis, sich während des Unterrichts auf dem Flur aufzuhalten*
dress code [ˈdres ˌkəʊd]	Kleiderordnung; Bekleidungsvorschriften
restroom *(AE)* [ˈrestrʊm]	Toilette

2

1 Word friends: American everyday life

Make pairs of two words and write them down.

school   code
mall   front   pass
middle   school
hall   high   yard
shopping   dress

1. _____
2. _____
3. _____
4. _____
5. _____
6. _____

2 What word?

Read the words in the phonetic alphabet and write them down. The grid on page 3 will help you.

1. [ɪmˈpreʃn]

   _____

2. [ˈhɔːlweɪ]

   _____

3. [ˈrestrʊm]

   _____

4. [ˈsʌbɜːb]

   _____

Station 1: Living here isn't bad

movie *(AE)* ['mu:vi]	Film
walk-in closet [ˌwɔ:kɪn 'klɒzɪt]	begehbarer Kleiderschrank
to **be around** [ˌbi: ə'raʊnd]	da sein; zusammen sein mit
not until [ˌnɒt ən'tɪl]	nicht vor; erst um/im
store *(AE)* [stɔ:]	Laden; Geschäft
drive [draɪv]	Fahrt; Anfahrt; Autofahrt
along for the ride [əˌlɒŋ fə ðə 'raɪd]	mit dabei
ride [raɪd]	Fahrt; Ritt
curfew ['kɜ:fju:]	Sperrstunde; Ausgangssperre
to **meet up** [ˌmi:t 'ʌp]	sich treffen
downtown *(AE)* [ˌdaʊn'taʊn]	im Stadtzentrum
to **get used to sth** [ˌget 'ju:zd tə]	sich an etw. gewöhnen
floor [flɔ:]	Stockwerk
elevator *(AE)* ['elɪveɪtə]	Aufzug; Lift
luckily ['lʌkɪli]	glücklicherweise
movie theater *(AE)* ['mu:vi ˌθɪətə]	Kino
soccer *(AE)* ['sɒkə]	Fußball
I'm afraid … [ˌaɪm ə'freɪd]	Leider …
to **keep in touch** [ˌki:p ɪn 'tʌtʃ]	in Kontakt bleiben
to **keep** [ki:p], **kept** [kept], **kept** [kept]	*hier:* weiter tun; immer wieder tun
no wonder [ˌnəʊ 'wʌndə]	kein Wunder
Pilgrim ['pɪlgrɪm]	Pilger/-in
to **practice a religion** [ˌpræktɪs ə rɪ'lɪdʒn]	eine Religion ausüben
survivor [sə'vaɪvə]	Überlebende/-r
Native American [ˌneɪtɪv ə'merɪkən]	Ureinwohner/-in Amerikas; Indianer/-in; indianisch

harvest ['hɑːvɪst]	Ernte
to give thanks [ˌɡɪv 'θæŋks]	danken
Indian ['ɪndiən]	Indianer/-in; indianisch
menu ['menjuː]	Speisekarte
dish [dɪʃ]	Gericht; Speise
instead of [ɪn'sted əv]	statt; anstatt; an Stelle von
social media [ˌsəʊʃl 'miːdiə]	soziale Netzwerke
to mind [maɪnd]	etwas dagegen haben; einem etwas ausmachen
in the middle of nowhere [ɪn ðə ˌmɪdl əv 'nəʊweə]	mitten im Nirgendwo
to find one's way around [ˌfaɪnd wʌnz 'weɪ əˈraʊnd]	sich zurechtfinden
to be tired of [bi 'taɪəd əv]	es müde sein (zu); es leid sein (zu); es satt haben (zu)
likes (pl) [laɪks]	Vorlieben
dislikes (pl) [dɪs'laɪks]	Abneigungen
to unpack [ʌn'pæk]	auspacken
to dislike [dɪs'laɪk]	nicht mögen
to dream [driːm], dreamt [dremt], dreamt [dremt]	träumen
to be crazy about [bi 'kreɪzi əbaʊt]	verrückt sein nach; abfahren auf
insecure [ˌɪnsɪ'kjʊə]	unsicher
foreground ['fɔːɡraʊnd]	Vordergrund

3 Say it in American English!

Write down the American English words for the British English ones.

1. football

   _____

2. film

   _____

3. shop

   _____

4. cinema

   _____

4 My new life in the US

Put the correct words in Matt's e-mail to his grandma.

Dear Grandma,

I really like Pittsburgh. We live in an apartment close to ⬜⬜⬜⬜⬜⬜⬜[n]⬜, on the 22nd (!) ⬜[l]⬜⬜⬜, so I spend a lot of time in the ⬜⬜⬜[a]⬜⬜⬜. [L]⬜⬜⬜⬜⬜⬜⬜,

there are shops and cafés super close to where I live.

I have to stop now, I'm ⬜⬜⬜⬜⬜⬜⬜.

My friends are waiting for me in front of the ⬜[o]⬜⬜⬜ ⬜⬜⬜⬜⬜⬜⬜.

Let's ⬜⬜[e]⬜⬜ ⬜⬜ ⬜⬜⬜⬜⬜

by e-mail!

Yours, Matt

5 Sophie calls Matt

Complete what Sophie says with the correct phrases. They're all new phrases in Station 1.

Hi Matt! How are you? I'm at my aunt and uncle's house – it's

_____. I'm so bored! At least it's

easy to _____ my _____

because there aren't many streets, so it's hard to get lost!

I _____ driving two hours to the next

mall. Luckily, we're moving to Pittsburgh soon – I'd never

_____ living in the country! There's only one

thing I _____ : Tom's Café. They have the

best ice cream in the world! _____ I had to

wait for 20 minutes yesterday to get my "chocolate surprise"!

6 Odd word out

Cross out the word that doesn't fit.

1. harvest | wheat | dish | curfew
2. keep in touch | meet up | give thanks | hang out with
3. trip | floor | drive | ride
4. foreground | elevator | stairs | floor
5. be tired of | dislike | be crazy about | hate

Station 2: That's the worst thing to do!

committee [kəˈmɪti]	Komitee; Ausschuss
8th-grader *(AE)* [ˈeɪtθˌgreɪdə]	Achtklässler/-in
period *(AE)* [ˈpɪəriəd]	Stunde; Unterrichtsstunde
geek [giːk]	Außenseiter/-in
What a … [ˈwɒt ə]	Was für ein/-e …
shopper [ˈʃɒpə]	Käufer/-in
child labor *(AE)* [ˌtʃaɪld ˈleɪbə]	Kinderarbeit
sweatshop [ˈswetʃɒp]	Ausbeuterbetrieb
to **demonstrate** [ˈdemənstreɪt]	demonstrieren
right [raɪt]	Recht
whether [ˈweðə]	ob
to **prefer** [prɪˈfɜː]	vorziehen
to **control** [kənˈtrəʊl]	kontrollieren; steuern
might [maɪt]	könnte/-n (vielleicht)
to **argue** [ˈɑːgjuː]	argumentieren; streiten
to **clean out** [ˌkliːn ˈaʊt]	ausräumen; entrümpeln
clothing drive [ˈkləʊðɪŋ ˌdraɪv]	Kleidersammlung
homeless shelter [ˈhəʊmləs ˌʃeltə]	Obdachlosenunterkunft
homeless [ˈhəʊmləs]	obdachlos
to **wish** [wɪʃ]	(sich) wünschen
to **donate** [dəˈneɪt]	spenden; stiften
benefit [ˈbenɪfɪt]	Vorteil; Nutzen; Unterstützung
pound [paʊnd]	Pfund *(Maßeinheit)*
item [ˈaɪtəm]	Gegenstand; Objekt
drop-off [ˈdrɒpɒf]	Abgabe

7 Matt's dilemma

Put in the missing words. The words in brackets are definitions that will help you.

1. In second _____ **(AE word for 'lesson')**, Matt is looking at different layouts with two of the most popular _____ **(students in the 8th year of school)**, Scott and Eva.

2. Scott and Eva think that Henry and Tyler are _____ **(persons who are different from most of the others)** because they demonstrate against _____ **(adults' work done by children)**.

3. Eva says that Henry and Tyler shout at the _____ **(people who buy something)** in the mall and adds that they want her and the others to write about children's _____ **(what people are allowed to do or say)** in the yearbook. But she _____ **(like better)** to write about fun things.

Story: Nightmare at the mall!

nightmare [ˈnaɪtmeə]	Alptraum
believable [bɪˈliːvəbl]	glaubwürdig
exaggerated [ɪɡˈzædʒreɪtɪd]	übertrieben
unrealistic [ˌʌnrɪəˈlɪstɪk]	unrealistisch
coincidence [kəʊˈɪnsɪdns]	Zufall
to **open** [ˈəʊpn]	eröffnen
to **sign** [saɪn]	unterschreiben; unterzeichnen
amazed [əˈmeɪzd]	erstaunt; verblüfft
scared [skeəd]	verängstigt; ängstlich
right [raɪt]	direkt
cheer [tʃɪə]	Jubel; Hurraruf
dizzy [ˈdɪzi]	schwindelig
down [daʊn]	nieder
to **escape (from)** [ɪˈskeɪp frəm]	fliehen; entfliehen; flüchten; entkommen
protester [ˈprəʊtestə]	Protestierende/-r; Demonstrant/-in
to **touch** [tʌtʃ]	berühren; antippen
troublemaker [ˈtrʌblmeɪkə]	Unruhestifter/-in
to **leave sb alone** [ˌliːv əˈləʊn]	jmdn. in Ruhe lassen
obvious [ˈɒbviəs]	offensichtlich
twice [twaɪs]	zweimal
mess [mes]	Unordnung; Durcheinander; Schweinerei
to **mix** [mɪks]	zusammenpassen

8 Adjectives for people and things

Write the adjectives in the correct part of the grid.

obvious   amazed   dizzy   believable   scared   unrealistic   exaggerated   confident

People can be ...	Things can be ...

9 Definitions

Put in the correct words.

1. Something that's easy to see or understand is

   _____.

2. A _____ is a scary dream.

3. If you run away from something, you

   _____ from it.

4. If you do something two times, you do it

   _____.

10 Word friends

Draw lines to match the verbs and nouns that are often used together.

1. open
2. sign
3. escape from
4. touch
5. tidy up

a) a mess
b) the ground
c) a store
d) a T-shirt or book
e) a crowd

11 Jumbled sentences

Find the right word order and make sentences.

1. to | I'm | stay | you | right | going | to | next

_____

2. and | Lena | feel | to | dizzy | started | sick

_____

3. prison | could | she | spending | imagine | night | in | easily | a

_____

_____

4. face | around | came | she | to | with | face | Matt | turned | and

_____

Action USA! Go on, text her!

Go on! [ˌgəʊ ˈɒn]	Los!
attractive [əˈtræktɪv]	attraktiv
boyfriend [ˈbɔɪfrend]	Freund *(in einer Paarbeziehung)*
attitude [ˈætɪtjuːd]	Haltung; Einstellung
to **overdo** [əʊvəˈduː], **overdid** [əʊvəˈdɪd], **overdone** [əʊvəˈdʌn]	übertreiben; zu weit gehen
date [deɪt]	Verabredung; Date

Skills: How to write in the appropriate style

content [ˈkɒntent]	Inhalt
toothpaste [ˈtuːθpeɪst]	Zahnpasta
ironic [aɪˈrɒnɪk]	ironisch
informative [ɪnˈfɔːmətɪv]	informativ
natural [ˈnætʃrl]	natürlich; Natur-
individual [ˌɪndɪˈvɪdʒuəl]	Einzelperson; Einzelne/-r; Individuum
pose [pəʊz]	Pose; Haltung
season [ˈsiːzn]	Saison; Jahreszeit
championship [ˈtʃæmpiənʃɪp]	Meisterschaft

Unit task: An American-style yearbook

double [ˈdʌbl]	Doppel-; zweimal
concert [ˈkɒnsət]	Konzert

12 Opposites

Find the opposite of each word.

1. group   _____

2. girlfriend   _____

3. background ↵ _____

4. to like ↵ _____

13 Yearbook texts

Put in the correct words.

`poses` `informative` `content` `overdo` `ironic`

A yearbook is divided into different sections, and each section has its own typical _____ and language tone. In 'Clubs and Sports', the style is _____ , in 'Student Superlatives' you can find _____ comments on funny _____ for photos too. But students shouldn't _____ it – they might hurt somebody's feelings.

14 Check on your ... AE vocabulary

Make a list of the American English words you've learned in Unit 2.

_____

_____

_____

_____

_____

TS 2

Text smart 2 Advertisements

> **Tip**
>
> Du kannst dein Englisch super üben, indem du immer mal wieder einen englischen Text liest. Such doch im Internet nach Artikeln aus englischsprachigen Zeitungen oder Zeitschriften zu einem Thema, das dich interessiert. Oder du liest eine Kurzgeschichte auf Englisch!

ad(vertisement) [əd'vɜːtɪsmənt]	Anzeige; Werbespot
product ['prɒdʌkt]	Produkt; Erzeugnis
just about anywhere [ˌdʒʌst əˌbaʊt 'enɪweə]	praktisch überall
advertiser ['ædvətaɪzə]	Werbefachmann/-frau
to win sb over [ˌwɪn 'əʊvə]	jmdn. für sich gewinnen; jmdn. überzeugen

Introduction

brand [brænd]	Marke
immediately [ɪ'miːdiətli]	sofort; gleich
to give away [ˌgɪv ə'weɪ]	verteilen; verschenken
sample ['sɑːmpl]	Probe; Muster
chocolate bar ['tʃɒklət ˌbɑː]	Schokoriegel
to fall for ['fɔːl fə]	hereinfallen auf
hair [heə]	Haar; Haare
to advertise ['ædvətaɪz]	Werbung machen; werben; anpreisen; inserieren
receptive [rɪ'septɪv]	empfänglich
temptation [temp'teɪʃn]	Versuchung
sceptical ['skeptɪkl]	skeptisch
advertising *(no pl)* ['ædvətaɪzɪŋ]	Werbung; Reklame

TS 2

1 Phrasal verbs

a) *Find the correct prepositions for the verbs and write down the phrasal verbs. Use each preposition only once.*

meet   give   rely   on   out   up
win   fall   clean   over   away   for

1. _____   4. _____

2. _____   5. _____

3. _____   6. _____

b) *Complete the text with the phrasal verbs from a).*

Advertisers try to _____ customers _____ in different ways.

They _____ free samples of a product, for example, and hope that people will _____ this trick. Or customers are told in ads that they should really _____ their closets in spring and then _____ with their friends in the mall to buy new outfits for the summer.

They _____ people wanting to be cool and modern!

Station: Did you see that new ad?

to **spice up** [ˌspaɪsˈʌp]	aufpeppen
highly [ˈhaɪli]	höchst-
brand-new [ˌbrændˈnjuː]	brandneu
available [əˈveɪləbl]	erhältlich; verfügbar
glamorous [ˈglæmrəs]	glamourös
lovely [ˈlʌvli]	schön; hübsch
nerd [nɜːd]	Nerd *(Person, die intelligent, aber sozial unbeholfen ist)*
target [ˈtɑːgɪt]	Ziel; Ziel-
eye-catcher [ˈaɪkætʃə]	Blickfang; Hingucker
visual [ˈvɪʒuəl]	Bild
ad copy [ˈæd ˌkɒpi]	Werbetext
image [ˈɪmɪdʒ]	Bild; Abbildung
billboard [ˈbɪlbɔːd]	Plakatwand
approach [əˈprəʊtʃ]	Herangehensweise; Vorgehensweise; Ansatz; Annäherung
truckload [ˈtrʌkləʊd]	Lastwagenladung
arrival [əˈraɪvl]	Ankommende/-r; Neuzugang
to **settle for less** [ˌsetl fə ˈles]	sich mit weniger zufrieden geben
effective [ɪˈfektɪv]	effektiv; wirkungsvoll
to **attract** [əˈtrækt]	anziehen
fabulous [ˈfæbjələs]	sagenhaft; fantastisch
effectiveness [ɪˈfektɪvnəs]	Effektivität; Wirksamkeit

Options

trash *(AE)* [træʃ]	Abfall; Müll
ugly [ˈʌgli]	hässlich

TS 2

2 Word search: Advertising

Find eight advertising words (→, ↓ or ↗) and complete the sentences with three of them.

X	G	N	A	D	C	O	P	Y	A
U	M	L	N	J	O	P	A	P	D
Y	S	A	M	P	L	E	L	R	V
Y	R	N	B	X	K	C	T	O	E
B	I	L	L	B	O	A	R	D	R
S	V	Z	I	R	W	Q	J	U	T
V	I	S	U	A	L	P	K	C	I
R	Z	U	T	E	W	B	S	T	S
I	M	A	G	E	N	H	D	G	E

1. Hey, look at that _____ next to the bus stop. That chocolate bar looks so nice!

2. I was given a free _____ of it at the supermarket yesterday. I really loved it …

3. I've never heard of the _____ before – maybe it's new in the US.

45

3 Verb into noun

Find the nouns that belong to the same word family as the verbs.

1. produce ➤ _____ _____

2. tempt ➤ _____

3. wish ➤ _____

4. advertise ➤ _____ _____

   _____

5. arrive ➤ _____

6. survive ➤ _____

4 Check on your ... adjectives

Make a list of adjectives that are useful for writing ads.

_____

_____

_____

_____

_____

_____

_____

_____

Across cultures 3 School life – dos and don'ts

> **Tip**
>
> Lerne deine Vokabeln ab und zu zusammen mit deinen Freunden. So könnt ihr euch gegenseitig abfragen oder auch Tipps geben, wie ihr euch schwierige Wörter am besten merkt. Das hilft euch nicht nur dabei, die Wörter gut zu können, sondern macht auch Spaß!

corridor [ˈkɒrɪdɔː]	Gang; Flur; Korridor
gym(nasium) [dʒɪm; dʒɪmˈneɪziəm]	Turnhalle
lab(oratory) [læb; ləˈbɒrətri]	Labor
cell phone *(AE)* [ˈselfəʊn]	Mobiltelefon; Handy
to **skip** [skɪp]	auslassen; schwänzen
to **cheat** [tʃiːt]	mogeln; betrügen
to **get caught** [ˌget ˈkɔːt]	erwischt werden; ertappt werden
principal *(AE)* [ˈprɪnsɪpl]	Schulleiter/-in
to **be suspended** [bi səˈspendɪd]	suspendiert werden; zeitweilig vom Unterricht ausgeschlossen werden
detention [dɪˈtenʃn]	Nachsitzen; Haft; Verhaftung
lunchtime [ˈlʌntʃtaɪm]	Mittagszeit; Mittagspause
to **complete** [kəmˈpliːt]	fertigstellen; vervollständigen; vollenden
consequence [ˈkɒnsɪkwəns]	Konsequenz; Folge
otherwise [ˈʌðəwaɪz]	sonst
to **stand in line** *(AE)* [ˌstænd ɪn ˈlaɪn]	anstehen; Schlange stehen; (sich) anstellen
to **switch off** [ˌswɪtʃ ˈɒf]	ausschalten
to **be about to do sth** [bi əˈbaʊt tə]	im Begriff sein, etw. zu tun

AC3

to **get into trouble** [ˌget ˌɪntə ˈtrʌbl]	in Schwierigkeiten geraten
so (that) [ˌsəʊ ˈðæt]	damit; so dass
cheat sheet [ˈtʃiːt ʃiːt]	Spickzettel
You'd better ... (= You had better) [ˈjuːd ˌbetə]	Du solltest lieber ...
If I were you ... [ˌɪf aɪ wɜː ˈjuː]	Wenn ich du wäre ...
No risk, no fun! [nəʊ ˌrɪsk nəʊ ˈfʌn]	Wer nicht wagt, der nicht gewinnt.
mad [mæd]	wütend
I can't see the point of ... [aɪ ˌkɑːnt siː ðə ˈpɔɪnt ˌəv]	Ich sehe keinen Sinn darin ...
waste [weɪst]	Verschwendung

1 Talking in English

Write down what you could say in the situations described. Use phrases that are new in Across cultures 3.

1. Your younger brother is listening to music instead of doing his homework.

   _____

2. Your best friend got a bad mark in a test and doesn't know how to tell his / her parents. He / She asks what you would do.

   _____

   _____

3. A classmate has said nasty things about you. Your friends think you should talk to him / her, but you think that's useless.

   _____

2 A crossword: School words

Put in the correct words and find the solution.

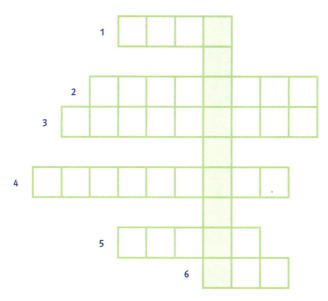

1. If you ... a class, you get into trouble.
2. American students aren't allowed to be in the ... without a hall pass.
3. If you break a rule several times, you can be ... .
4. Students who forget to do their homework very often might get ... .
5. If you ... on a test, you'll probably get a bad mark.
6. In Science lessons, students often work in the ... .

Solution:

A _____ is the "boss" of an American school.

Unit 3 City of dreams: New York

> **Tip**
>
> Du kannst deinen Wortschatz ganz einfach erweitern:
> Sieh dir z. B. deinen Lieblingsfilm auf Englisch an.
> So lernst du Redewendungen für Unterhaltungen!
> Je öfter du Filme auf Englisch anschaust, umso besser
> wirst du die Schauspieler verstehen.

Introduction

intersection [ˌɪntəˈsekʃn]	Kreuzung
district [ˈdɪstrɪkt]	Distrikt; Bezirk
lung [lʌŋ]	Lunge
a pocketful of [ə ˈpɒkɪtfl ˌəv]	Unmengen von/an
gonna (= going to) *(coll)* [ˈgɒnə]	wird/werden
to **make it** [ˈmeɪk ˌɪt]	es schaffen
by any means [baɪ ˌenɪ ˈmiːnz]	mit allen Mitteln
to **inspire** [ɪnˈspaɪə]	inspirieren; anregen
melting pot [ˈmeltɪŋ ˌpɒt]	Schmelztiegel
jungle [ˈdʒʌŋgl]	Dschungel

3

1 Word friends: New York

Find the missing words in the noun pairs and write them down.

1. _____ pot

2. concrete _____

3. theater _____

2 Definitions

Put in the correct words.

1. An _____ is a place where two or more roads meet.

2. If you want to say 'a lot of', you can also say '_____'.

3. A person or an event _____ you if it gives you the idea for something, e.g. for a song.

4. A _____ is a place where people from different origins come together to live and form a new culture.

5. A _____ is a forest with a very hot climate.

Station 1: Saving the best for last

to **save the best for last** [ˌseɪv ðə ˌbest fə ˈlɑːst]	sich das Beste bis zum Schluss aufheben
to **take the day off** [ˌteɪk ðə ˌdeɪ ˈɒf]	sich den Tag freinehmen
diner *(AE)* [ˈdaɪnə]	einfaches Restaurant mit Theke und Tischen
conference [ˈkɒnfrns]	Konferenz; Tagung
guidebook [ˈgaɪdbʊk]	Reiseführer
to **gasp** [gɑːsp]	tief Luft holen; keuchen
classical [ˈklæsɪkl]	klassisch
bank [bæŋk]	Bank
sculpture [ˈskʌlptʃə]	Skulptur
since [sɪns]	da
naked [ˈneɪkɪd]	nackt
for free [fə ˈfriː]	umsonst; kostenlos
on a shoestring [ˌɒn ə ˈʃuːstrɪŋ]	für/mit wenig Geld
to **time** [taɪm]	den richtigen Zeitpunkt wählen
block [blɒk]	Block; Häuserblock
enthusiasm [ɪnˈθjuːziæzm]	Enthusiasmus; Begeisterung
just in time [ˌdʒʌst ɪn ˈtaɪm]	gerade rechtzeitig
sunset [ˈsʌnset]	Sonnenuntergang
to **sneak** [sniːk], **snuck** [snʌk], **snuck** [snʌk]	schleichen; schmuggeln
service [ˈsɜːvɪs]	Service; Dienstleistung; Dienst
Leave that to me. [ˌliːv ðæt tə ˈmiː]	Überlass das mir.
bright [braɪt]	hell; leuchtend; strahlend
tour company [ˈtʊə ˌkʌmpəni]	Reiseanbieter
to **be located** [bi ləʊˈkeɪtɪd]	gelegen sein; liegen
subway *(AE)* [ˈsʌbweɪ]	U-Bahn
to **groan** [grəʊn]	stöhnen

statue [ˈstætʃuː]	Statue; Standbild
liberty [ˈlɪbəti]	Freiheit
artist [ˈɑːtɪst]	Künstler/-in
tablet [ˈtæblət]	Tafel
spike [spaɪk]	Spitze; Stachel
to **base on** [ˈbeɪs ˌɒn]	stützen auf
goddess [ˈgɒdes]	Göttin
to **be known as** [bi ˈnəʊn ˌəz]	bekannt sein als
enlightenment [ɪnˈlaɪtnmənt]	Aufklärung; Erleuchtung
ethnic [ˈeθnɪk]	ethnisch; Volks-; *hier:* exotisch
from the outside [ˌfrəm ðɪ ˌaʊtˈsaɪd]	von außen
delicious [dɪˈlɪʃəs]	köstlich
fried [fraɪd]	gebraten *(in der Pfanne)*
pastry [ˈpeɪstri]	Teig; Teigtasche
filling [ˈfɪlɪŋ]	Füllung
Jewish [ˈdʒuːɪʃ]	jüdisch
truck *(AE)* [trʌk]	*hier:* Wagen
cart [kɑːt]	Karren
New Yorker [ˌnjuːˈjɔːkə]	New Yorker/-in
to **combine** [kəmˈbaɪn]	kombinieren; verbinden
flavor *(AE)* [ˈfleɪvə]	Geschmack; Aroma
specialty *(AE)* [ˈspeʃlti]	Spezialität; Besonderheit
combination [ˌkɒmbɪˈneɪʃn]	Kombination; Verbindung
hometown [ˈhəʊmtaʊn]	Heimatstadt
spot [spɒt]	Fleck; Ort

3

3 Find the missing word

Put in the missing words.

1. London – Underground   New York – _____

2. house – architect   sculpture – _____

3. United States – states   New York – _____

4. money – bank   food / drinks – _____

4 In New York

Complete the words. They're all new in Station 1.

If you're out and about in New York on

a s _ _ _ _ _ _ _ _ _

and you're hungry, you can either go

to a d _ _ _ _ or buy a hot dog or

bagel from a food t _ _ _ _ or c _ _ _.

Or what about a samosa – a

f _ _ _ _ p _ _ _ _ _ with a

vegetarian filling? In New York, you

can find e _ _ _ _ _ food from all

over the world. And New Yorkers are really creative in inventing new

food c _ _ _ _ _ _ _ _ _ _ _. What do you think about a

cronut?!

5 What can you say?

You're visiting your aunt in New York. Write down what you say in English.

1. Du sagst, dass es super ist, dass sie sich den Tag freigenommen hat.

   _____

   _____

   _____

2. Du fragst, wo das Empire State Building liegt.

   _____

   _____

   _____

3. Du erzählst, dass du gelesen hast, dass Bedloe Island jetzt als „Liberty Island" bekannt ist.

   _____

   _____

   _____

4. In einem Diner sagst du, dass das Essen wirklich köstlich ist und dass ihr euch das Beste bis zum Schluss aufgehoben habt.

   _____

   _____

   _____

Station 2: Life is a trip

to **lift** [lɪft]	heben; hochheben; anheben
trunk *(AE)* [trʌŋk]	Kofferraum
to **be done with** [bi 'dʌn wɪð]	fertig sein mit
break [breɪk]	Durchbruch
rejection [rɪ'dʒektʃn]	Ablehnung; Absage
to **come true** [ˌkʌm 'truː]	wahr werden; in Erfüllung gehen
good luck [ˌgʊd 'lʌk]	(viel) Glück
sidewalk *(AE)* ['saɪdwɔːk]	Gehweg; Gehsteig
businessman ['bɪznɪsmæn]	Geschäftsmann
not necessarily [ˌnɒt nesə'serəli]	nicht notwendigerweise; nicht unbedingt
however [haʊ'evə]	jedoch
bill *(AE)* [bɪl]	Geldschein; Rechnung
change [tʃeɪndʒ]	Münzgeld; Wechselgeld
to **get in** [ˌget ˌ'ɪn]	einsteigen
yet [jet]	doch; und trotzdem; und dennoch
to **complain** [kəm'pleɪn]	sich beschweren; sich beklagen
to **shop** [ʃɒp]	einkaufen; shoppen
needless to say [ˌniːdləs tə 'seɪ]	natürlich; selbstverständlich
tip [tɪp]	Trinkgeld
grade *(AE)* [greɪd]	Note
busker ['bʌskə]	Straßenmusikant/-in
to **perform** [pə'fɔːm]	aufführen; auftreten
freeway *(AE)* ['friːweɪ]	Autobahn
to **transport** [træn'spɔːt]	transportieren; befördern
lorry ['lɒri]	Lastwagen
to **fail to do sth** ['feɪl tə]	versäumen, etw. zu tun; es nicht schaffen, etw. zu tun
rags to riches [ˌrægz tə ˌ'rɪtʃɪz]	vom Tellerwäscher zum Millionär

to **make a living (from)** [ˌmeɪk ə ˈlɪvɪŋ frəm]	seinen Lebensunterhalt bestreiten (mit)
either … or … [ˈaɪðə/ˈiːðə … ɔː]	entweder … oder …

6 Money, money, money

Put in the correct 'money' words.

1. The first guest at the Diner paid with a large

   _____, so Diego had almost no

   _____ left.

2. He was given a big _____ from the

   businessman who had just come in for a coffee.

3. He was very happy about that because his parents couldn't

   give him very much _____.

   Most of his friends were getting much more every month.

4. Sometimes guests from abroad wanted to pay in foreign

   _____.

   But Diego's boss didn't want

   him to accept these.

7 Bye bye, Lea!

Put in the correct verbs in the correct tense.

complain | come true | inspire | shop | lift | perform | gasp | get in

Rylee's dad _____ Lea's suitcase into the trunk of his car. They all _____ and drove to the airport. "It's sad I have to leave," Lea said. "But my dream _____: I've been to New York!" "Look at that busker," Rylee said. "It must be hard to _____ on the street every day." Rylee's mum smiled: "So you two have no reason to _____, do you? You do well at school, and you've got pocket money so that you can go downtown to _____ …" Suddenly they saw the Statue of Liberty right in front of them in the sunset. Lea _____. "That's a great view to say goodbye to New York," she said. "Maybe it _____ you to write a poem," Rylee's dad joked. "Why not?" Lea answered, and she was serious.

Story: Asphalt Tribe

panel ['pænl]	Bild *(eines Comics)*
lead-in ['li:dɪn]	Einführung; Einleitung
shape [ʃeɪp]	Form
sequence ['si:kwəns]	Abfolge; Reihenfolge
consecutive [kən'sekjʊtɪv]	aufeinanderfolgend; fortlaufend
to **overlap** [ˌəʊvə'læp]	(sich) überlappen
to **lay** [leɪ], **laid** [leɪd], **laid** [leɪd]	legen
to **make use of** [meɪk 'ju:z əv]	benutzen; verwenden
long shot ['lɒŋ ʃɒt]	Totale *(Kameraeinstellung)*
medium shot ['mi:diəm ʃɒt]	Halbtotale *(Kameraeinstellung)*
medium ['mi:diəm]	mittel; mittelgroß
effect [ɪ'fekt]	Effekt; Wirkung
stylistic [staɪ'lɪstɪk]	Stil-; stilistisch
speed [spi:d]	Geschwindigkeit

8 Say it in a different way

Write down the missing word or phrase to make a sentence with a similar meaning.

1. This car is driving very fast.

   → This car is driving at high _____.

2. I like the introduction to the story.

   → I like the _____ to the story.

3. They put their raincoats on the bed.

   → They _____ their raincoats

   on the bed.

9 Graphic novels

Put in the correct words.

A graphic novel is divided into individual _____ which can be of different sizes and _____. But the story is not only told by pictures, but also by speech or thought bubbles and _____. Sometimes the panels are not arranged consecutively, but they _____. This special _____ makes graphic novels interesting to read, just like the different kinds of shots. There can be _____ or _____ shots and close-ups. All of them have different _____ – some create suspense, for example; others make the reader experience the story.

10 Synonyms

Write down a word with the same or a similar meaning.

1. picture _____
2. to stage _____
3. to buy _____

Action USA! New Yorkers don't do things like that!

to **cringe** [krɪndʒ]	schaudern; sich ducken
unexpected [ˌʌnɪkˈspektɪd]	unerwartet

Skills: How to conduct a podcast interview

to **conduct** [kənˈdʌkt]	durchführen; ausführen
path [pɑːθ]	Pfad; Weg
follow-up [ˈfɒləʊʌp]	Fortsetzung; Folge-
talk [tɔːk]	Gespräch; Unterhaltung

11 Word families: Questions and answers

Complete the sentences with a word from the same word family.

1. Did you **expect** your grandparents today? – No, it was an

   _____ visit!

2. In your _____, remember to ask

   Daniel Radcliffe about the Quidditch scenes. – Good idea!

   A question like that should immediately **follow** the small talk

   at the beginning.

3. The students I interviewed **talked** a lot about their problems

   with cyber bullying. – So it was really important that you held

   this _____ !

4. You used interesting **stylistic** elements in your text. – OK!

   Do you think I need to improve the _____

   of the text in any way?

12 Phrases for interviews

Write down two phrases each for the different stages of an interview.

1. Small talk: _____

2. Follow-up: _____

3. Getting specific: _____

4. Open questions: _____

5. At the end: _____

13 Check on your … AE spelling

Write down the AE words you've learned so far that are spelled differently from the BE spelling.

Text smart 3 Internet texts

> **Tip**
>
> Wenn du dir bei der Aussprache bestimmter Wörter nicht sicher bist, schlage sie in einem Online-Wörterbuch nach. Denn dort kannst du dir auch die Aussprache anhören – in BE und AE.

Introduction

reliable [rɪˈlaɪəbl]	verlässlich; zuverlässig; vertrauenswürdig
inconvenient [ˌɪnkənˈviːniənt]	unbequem; lästig
up-to-date [ˌʌptəˈdeɪt]	modern; zeitgemäß; aktuell
tutorial [tjuːˈtɔːriəl]	Tutorium; Tutorial
moon landing [ˈmuːn ˌlændɪŋ]	Mondlandung
science [saɪəns]	Wissenschaft; Naturwissenschaft
astronaut [ˈæstrənɔːt]	Astronaut/-in
human [ˈhjuːmən]	Mensch
to **be considered (to be)** sth [bɪ kənˈsɪdəd tə]	als etw. gelten

TS 3

1 Internet vocabulary

Draw lines to match the verbs and nouns or phrases that are often used together.

1. watch   a) up-to-date on social media
2. post   b) quick information with apps
3. stay   c) blogs
4. get   d) research for school projects on science websites
5. do   e) a comment
6. follow   f) tutorials

2 Odd word out

Cross out the word that doesn't fit.

1. human | person | machine | man
2. up-to-date | reliable | inconvenient | sequence
3. astronaut | panel | moon landing | rock
4. effect | tutorial | blog | social media website
5. science | discovery | talk | invention
6. speed | fast | quick | shape
7. medium | small | media | large
8. freeway | path | road | street

Station 1: An online wiki text

wiki (text)	['wɪki ˌtekst]	Wikitext
mission	['mɪʃn]	Mission; Auftrag
to touch down	[tʌtʃ 'daʊn]	landen
surface	['sɜːfɪs]	Oberfläche
to announce	[əˈnaʊns]	ankündigen; durchsagen
to step	[step]	treten; steigen
president	['prezɪdnt]	Präsident/-in
priority	[praɪˈɒrəti]	Priorität; Vorrang
to challenge	['tʃælɪndʒ]	herausfordern
engineer	[ˌendʒɪˈnɪə]	Ingenieur/-in; Techniker/-in
political	[pəˈlɪtɪkl]	politisch
hoax	[həʊks]	Täuschung; Trick
conspiracy	[kənˈspɪrəsi]	Verschwörung
theory	['θɪəri]	Theorie
to stage	[steɪdʒ]	inszenieren; aufführen
the public	[ðə ˈpʌblɪk]	die Öffentlichkeit
to involve	[ɪnˈvɒlv]	involvieren; einbeziehen; beteiligen
cover-up	[ˈkʌvərʌp]	Vertuschung
government	[ˈgʌvnmənt]	Regierung
complicated	[ˈkɒmplɪkeɪtɪd]	kompliziert
impossible	[ɪmˈpɒsəbl]	unmöglich
to make sense	[ˌmeɪk ˈsens]	Sinn ergeben; einleuchten
at the time	[ˌət ðə ˈtaɪm]	damals
to run	[rʌn]	betreiben; leiten; führen
tech	[tek]	Technologie; Technik
respect	[rɪˈspekt]	Respekt
entertaining	[ˌentəˈteɪnɪŋ]	unterhaltsam
function	[ˈfʌŋkʃn]	Funktion
to trick	[trɪk]	austricksen; täuschen

to **estimate** [ˈestɪmeɪt]	schätzen
to **question** [ˈkwestʃən]	fragen; hinterfragen
critical [ˈkrɪtɪkl]	kritisch

3 What do they do?

Complete the descriptions with the correct jobs.

1. An _____ invents new machines or computer programmes.

2. A _____ is the head of state or the head of a company.

3. A _____ does research to make new discoveries in medicine or biology, for example.

4. An _____ creates print, online or TV ads for new products.

5. A _____ interviews people and writes articles.

4 Wiki text vs. blog post

Write the words or phrases in the correct part of the grid.

entertaining   factual   plays a trick on somebody

questions somebody's motivations   informative

stages a hoax   reliable   believable

Wiki text	Blog post

5 Opposites

Find the opposite of each word.

1. possible   _____

2. boring   _____

3. beautiful   _____

4. animal   _____

Station 2: Online ratings

to **rate** [reɪt]	bewerten; einstufen
space [speɪs]	Weltraum; Weltall
space program ['speɪs ˌprəʊgræm]	Raumfahrtprogramm
breathtaking ['breθˌteɪkɪŋ]	atemberaubend
well-written [ˌwel'rɪtn]	gut geschrieben
disappointing [ˌdɪsə'pɔɪntɪŋ]	enttäuschend
special effect [ˌspeʃl ɪ'fekt]	Spezialeffekt
well-developed [ˌweldɪ'veləpt]	gut entwickelt; ausgereift
undeveloped [ˌʌndɪ'veləpt]	unentwickelt; unausgereift
badly-written [ˌbædli'rɪtn]	schlecht geschrieben
weak [wiːk]	schwach

6 Make new words

Use the prefixes or suffixes to form adjectives.

Prefixes: dis- | un- | in- | im- | -y | -less

Words: developed | honest | possible | luck | secure | realistic | expected | health | use | end

1. _____
2. _____
3. _____
4. _____
5. _____
6. _____
7. _____
8. _____
9. _____
10. _____

7 An online rating

Put in the correct words.

`breathtaking` `weak` `special effects` `well-developed` `believable` `space`

Lost on the Moon is the best movie set in

_____ I've ever seen. It's full of

action, suspense and _____.

_____ characters make

the story _____, and

_____ visuals hooked me

from the first minute. Only the costumes are rather

_____ – they should definitely be

more up-to date.

8 Check on your … science vocabulary

Make a list of the science words you've learned in Text smart 3. Then add those from Green Line 3 *and* 4.

_____

_____

_____

_____

AC 4

Across cultures 4 What you say and how you say it

> **Tip**
>
> Sprich dir deine Vokabeln ab und zu laut vor, oder lass sie dir von Freunden, Geschwistern oder deinen Eltern vorlesen. So kannst du sie dir noch besser merken.

register [ˈredʒɪstə]	Sprachebene; Register
Canadian [kəˈneɪdiən]	kanadisch; Kanadier/-in
to **pronounce** [prəˈnaʊns]	aussprechen
schedule *(AE)* [ˈʃedjuːl; ˈskedʒuːl]	Stundenplan; Fahrplan; Terminkalender
though [ðəʊ]	doch; jedoch; obwohl
water fountain [ˈwɔːtə ˌfaʊntɪn]	Wasserspender
informal [ɪnˈfɔːml]	informell; zwanglos
nope *(infml)* [nəʊp]	nee; nö
It sucks. *(slang)* [ɪt ˈsʌks]	Das ist zum Kotzen.
ain't (= isn't/aren't) [eɪnt]	ist nicht; sind nicht
totally [ˈtəʊtli]	völlig; total
whatever [wɒtˈevə]	was/wie auch immer; egal (was/welche)
no more [ˌnəʊ ˈmɔː]	nicht mehr
(I) didn't mean to ... [aɪ ˌdɪdnt ˈmiːn tə]	Ich wollte nicht ...
auntie [ˈɑːnti]	Tantchen
not ... either [nɒt ... ˈaɪðə; nɒt ... ˈiːðə]	auch nicht
to **mind sth** [maɪnd]	auf etw. aufpassen

AC 4

1 Which register?

Put in the correct phrase in the correct register.

It's so wild to see you again | it sucks | I don't go there anymore

It was, like, so totally not my thing | I'm sorry

1. **Old lady:** Be careful, young man! You just stepped on my foot!

   Boy: Oh, _____.

2. **Girl:** I don't want to do that Maths homework. It's too much!

   Boy: Yeah, _____!

3. **Callum:** Did you like the film we watched last night?

   Tristan: Nope. _____.

4. **Tristan's grandad:** I think you need to leave now for your soccer training.

   Tristan: _____.

   I've started to play baseball and I like it better!

5. **Sophie:** Hi Matt! What's up?

   Matt: Hi! _____!

AC 4

2 Pronunciation: AE or BE?

Read the words in the phonetic alphabet and write them down. Add if they're AE or BE too.

1. [nuːz] _____ ___

2. [dɒg] _____ ___

3. [noʊ] _____ ___

4. [bɑːθ] _____ ___

5. [wɜːrk] _____ ___

6. [æsk] _____ ___

3 Where are they from?

Make adjectives from the country names and use them to complete the sentences.

Britain   Germany   the US   France   Canada

1. Many ice hockey players in Germany are _____.

2. The players of the _____ national football team usually wear white shirts.

3. _____ cheese is famous all over the world.

4. Most _____ students take the Pledge of Allegiance every morning.

5. _____ students are used to wearing school uniforms.

Solutions

Unit 1

1 Find the word
1. passenger 2. arrivals hall 3. seasick 4. currency
5. suitcase
Solution: plane

2 Rhymes
1. shutter 2. coast 3. soup 4. sleep 5. spill 6. style

3 Say it in a different way
1. Hang on 2. abroad 3. addict 4. your sister called
5. sleep now 6. style 7. big deal

4 Word friends
1. vending machine 2. arrivals hall 3. immigration office
4. flight attendant 5. side room

5 Airport words
Lösungsvorschlag:

People at the airport: flight attendant, pilot, passenger, traveller
Places at the airport: arrivals hall, departure lounge, immigration office, customs

6 A refugee's story
overloaded, crushed, steady, depressing, homesick

7 Mixed bag: Travel words
1. ferry, rocked, seasick 2. checkpoints, passport, official
3. take-off, landing, air-conditioning

8 Odd word out
1. mask 2. invisible 3. concrete 4. truth 5. realistic

9 Film genres
1. c) 2. a) 3. d) 4. b)

10 Check on your … adjectives for a person's character
Lösungsvorschlag:

friendly, outgoing, nice, boring, cool, easy-going, strange, silly, rude, funny, quiet, clever, crazy, laid-back, creative, confident, competitive, honest, bossy, messy, optimistic, smart

11 What can you say?
1. The other day, I went to an Egyptian restaurant with my parents.
2. We talked to the boss and his son and it turned out that his son, Ahmed, is at my school.
3. Ahmed is my Arab friend.

Across cultures 1

1 Good manners or not?
Good manners: hold the door open for others, say 'please' and 'thank you', say hello back, smile at others
Bad manners: talk with your mouth full, point at somebody, stand in the way, litter the park

Text smart 1

1 What a director says …
1. stage 2. get into 3. identify with 4. entertain 5. mess up

2 Opposites
1. devil 2. tonight / this evening 3. unsure 4. unreal
5. outgoing 6. useless

3 Definitions
1. motive 2. white lie 3. pushy 4. arguments 5. mean

4 Mixed bag: Claire's thoughts
warned, Let's face it, dishonest, tempting, sensible, do well

5 Describe feelings and behaviour
1. shocked 2. guilty 3. tolerant 4. dishonest

6 Jumbled sentences
1. Our phone is out of order.
2. There's no need to worry.
3. One lie always leads to another.

7 Check on your … irregular verbs
Individuelle Lösung

Across cultures 2

1 Contrasts in the US
1. urban, rural 2. wealthy, poor 3. densely, sparsely

2 Word groups: Rural or urban?
In the city: crowded, parks, taxi, skyscraper, Broadway plays, densely populated, noisy
In the country: endless, corn, scenery, wheat, redwood tree, cactus, tractor

3 That's the US!
European, cultural, awesome, extreme, harsh, rural

Unit 2

1 Word friends: American everyday life
1. middle school 2. high school 3. dress code
4. hall pass 5. front yard 6. shopping mall

2 What word?
1. impression 2. hallway 3. restroom 4. suburb

3 Say it in American English!
1. soccer 2. movie 3. store 4. movie theater

4 My new life in the US
downtown, floor, elevator, Luckily, afraid, movie theater, keep in touch

5 Sophie calls Matt
in the middle of nowhere, find, way around, 'm / am tired of, get used to, 'm / am crazy about, No wonder

6 Odd word out
1. curfew 2. give thanks 3. floor 4. foreground
5. be crazy about

7 Matt's dilemma
1. period, 8th-graders 2. geeks, child labor
3. shoppers, rights, prefers

Solutions

8 Adjectives for people and things
People can be: amazed, dizzy, scared, confident
Things can be: obvious, believable, unrealistic, exaggerated

9 Definitions
1. obvious 2. nightmare 3. escape 4. twice

10 Word friends
1. c) 2. d) 3. e) 4. b) 5. a)

11 Jumbled sentences
1. I'm going to stay right next to you.
2. Lena started to feel sick and dizzy / dizzy and sick.
3. She could easily imagine spending a night in prison.
4. She turned around and came face to face with Matt.

12 Opposites
1. individual 2. boyfriend 3. foreground 4. to dislike

13 Yearbook texts
content, informative, ironic, poses, overdo

14 Check on your … AE vocabulary
front yard, middle school, high school, restroom, movie, store, downtown, elevator, movie theater, soccer, 8th-grader, period, child labor

Text smart 2

1 Phrasal verbs
a) 1. meet up 2. win over 3. rely on 4. fall for
   5. clean out 6. give away
b) win, over, give away, fall for, clean out, meet up, rely on

2 Word search: Advertising

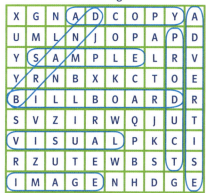

1. billboard 2. sample 3. brand

3 Verb into noun

1. product, production 2. temptation 3. wish 4. advertiser, advertisement, advertising 5. arrival 6. survivor

4 Check on your ... adjectives

Lösungsvorschlag:
brand-new, glamorous, lovely, fabulous, great, super, amazing, awesome

Across cultures 3

1 Talking in English

1. You'd better do your homework!
2. If I were you, I would tell my parents and promise to study more for the next test.
3. I can't see the point of talking to him / her.

2 A crossword: School words

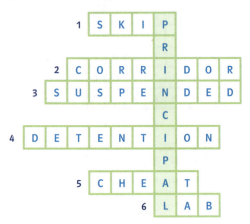

Solution: principal

Unit 3

1 Word friends: New York
1. melting 2. jungle 3. district

2 Definitions
1. intersection 2. a pocketful of 3. inspires 4. melting pot 5. jungle

3 Find the missing word
1. subway 2. artist 3. districts 4. diner

4 In New York
shoestring, diner, truck, cart, fried, pastry, ethnic, combinations

5 What can you say?
1. It's great you've taken the day off.
2. Where's the Empire State Building located?
3. I've read that Bedloe Island is now known as 'Liberty Island'.
4. The food is really delicious. We've saved the best for last!

6 Money, money, money
1. bill, change 2. tip 3. pocket money 4. currencies

7 Bye bye, Lea!
lifted, got in, has come true, perform, complain, shop, gasped, will inspire

8 Say it in a different way
1. speed 2. lead-in 3. laid

9 Graphic novels
panels, shapes, captions, overlap, sequence, long, medium, effects

10 Synonyms
1. panel 2. to perform 3. to shop

11 Word families: Questions and answers
1. unexpected 2. follow-up 3. talk 4. style

12 Phrases for interviews
1. This is a beautiful office. / Where did you grow up?
2. Can you tell me more about …? / Can you explain that to me?
3. How many …? / When did you …?
4. What do you think about …? / What are your goals?
5. Thanks, I enjoyed talking to you. / Thank you for this interesting talk.

13 Check on your … AE spelling
to symbolize, theater, labor, flavor, specialty, to realize, to practice, traveling, center, neighborhood

Text smart 3

1 Internet vocabulary
1. f) 2. e) 3. a) 4. b) 5. d) 6. c)

2 Odd word out
1. machine 2. sequence 3. panel 4. effect 5. talk 6. shape 7. media 8. path

Solutions

3 What do they do?
1. engineer 2. president 3. scientist 4. advertiser
5. reporter

4 Wiki text vs. blog post
Wiki text: factual, informative, reliable, believable
Blog post: entertaining, plays a trick on somebody, questions somebody's motivations, stages a hoax

5 Opposites
1. impossible 2. entertaining / interesting 3. ugly 4. human

6 Make new words
1. undeveloped 2. dishonest 3. impossible 4. lucky
5. insecure 6. unrealistic 7. unexpected 8. healthy
9. useless 10. endless

7 An online rating
space, special effects, Well-developed, believable, breathtaking, weak

8 Check on your ... science vocabulary
moon landing, science, astronaut, engineer, tech, space, space program; **Green Line 3:** invention, discovery, to clone, scientist, to invent, penicillin, steam engine

Across cultures 4

1 Which register?
1. I'm sorry
2. it sucks
3. It was, like, so totally not my thing
4. I don't go there anymore
5. It's so wild to see you again

2 Pronunciation: AE or BE?
1. news, AE 2. dog, BE 3. know, AE 4. bath, BE
5. work, AE 6. ask, AE

3 Where are they from?
1. Canadian 2. German 3. French 4. US / American 5. British